I0162192

Contemporary Aural Course
Preparatory set

by Margaret Brandman

Exclusive Distributors for Australia and New Zealand
Encore Music Distributors
227 Napier St
Fitzroy 3065 Victoria
Australia
Ph +61 3 9415 6677
Facsimile 61 3 9415 6655
Email sales@encoremusic.com.au

This book © Copyright 2019 by Margaret Brandman
trading as Jazzem Music
46 Gerrale St, Cronulla NSW 2230 Australia
ISBN **978-0-949683-02-1**
Order Nos:
Book: MMP 8069
Audio: MMP 8070
International Copyright Secured (APRA/AMCOS) All Rights Reserved

Cover designed by Camilla Done at Done Art & Design

Unauthorised reproduction of any part of this publication by any means including
photocopying is an infringement of copyright.

Contemporary Aural Course
Preparatory Set

Introduction

Welcome to the Contemporary Aural Course audio and book series.

The aims of this course are to give the student skills in Aural Discrimination, both away from the written music, and/or on the written page.

This will help the practical musician translate the sounds on the page to the sounds heard by the inner ear, before they are sounded on the instrument. It will also help musicians who wish to transcribe the sounds they hear from an audio source, or from their inner ear, into written music.

In this Preparatory Set of the course, students will be able to develop the skills required to handle the faster pace of Set One. Examples of the types of questions to be found and the skills required for Set One, will be presented at a slow to moderate pace. Younger people and novice musicians may like to limit their listening to one or two questions per session, rather than completing an entire lesson in one sitting.

Each lesson presents both listening sections for aural training and questions on the topics being covered. Throughout the course, there is an emphasis on the use of the voice to discern the sounds being heard. Students are encouraged to sing the pitches and songs wherever possible.

To fully understand the concepts covered in this course, I recommend the background theory required for this level be completed using the integrated books:
Contemporary Theory Primer and *Contemporary Theory Workbook – Book 1*.

This set of the course is designed to complement the Margaret Brandman piano method books: *Junior Primer* and *Contemporary Piano Method Book 1A* as well as *Playing Made Easy for Recorder* method book.

I trust you will find this Preparatory Set provides an easy and enjoyable introduction to Ear-training and the skills required for the higher levels of the course.
Download a free track listing from the Preparatory Aural page on the website and keep a note of the audio track alongside each written question.

The audio files for this set can be purchased from the order page at
www.margaretbrandman.com

Margaret S. Brandman
Diploma of Excellence (Dip.E) WPTA,
F.Mus.Ed.ASMC., F.Comp.ASMC., L.Perf.ASMC
Ph/D. (Mus/Arts) Trinity,. Hon D.L (IBC)
Hon.FNMSM (UK),. B. Mus. Syd (composition)
T. Mus.A. (piano)., A. Mus.A. (piano)

Contents

Topic   **Page**

Lesson One – Pitch

Refer to: Contemporary Theory Primer - Page 7
Contemporary Theory Workbook: Book 1 - Lesson 2

CD1 #8

Question One

Use **L** for Low, **M** for Middle and **H** for High.

Answers: (1) ……….   (2) ……….   (3) ……….   (4) ……….

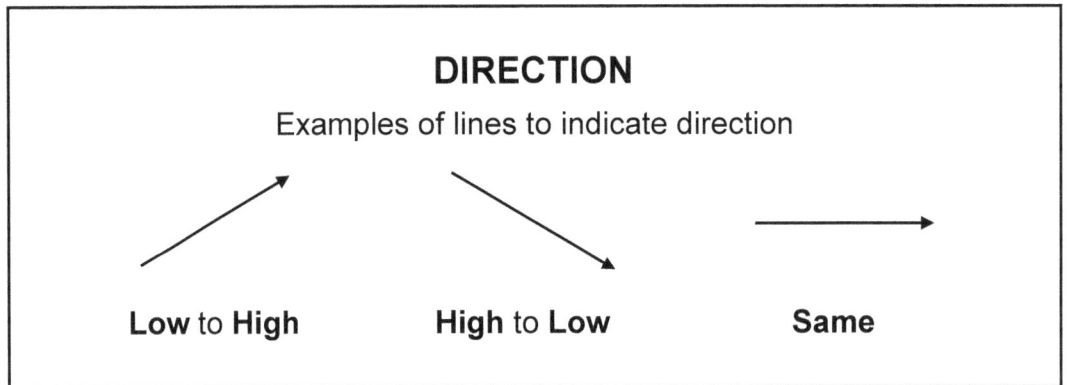

DIRECTION
Examples of lines to indicate direction

Low to **High**   **High** to **Low**   **Same**

CD1 #11

Question Two

Draw lines to show the direction in which sounds are moving.

Answers: (1) …………..   (2) …………..   (3) …………..

(4)…………..   (5) …………..   (6) …………..

CD1 #12

Question Three

Use **H** for higher and **L** for lower.

Answers: (1) ……….   (2) ……….   (3) ……….   (4) ……….

CD1 # 13

Question Four

Answers: (1) …………..   (2) …………..   (3) …………..

(4)…………..   (5) …………..   (6) …………..

Extra Practice Page

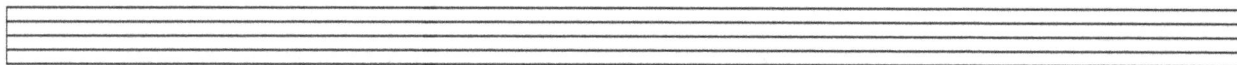

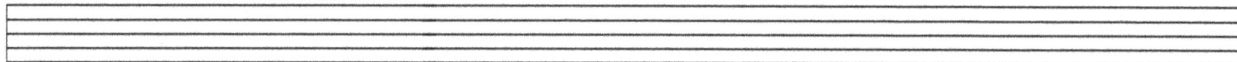

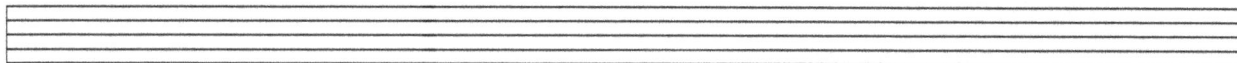

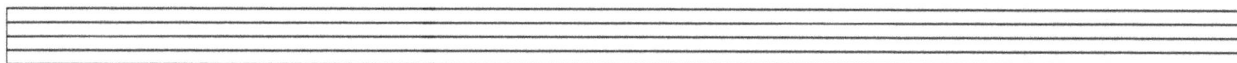

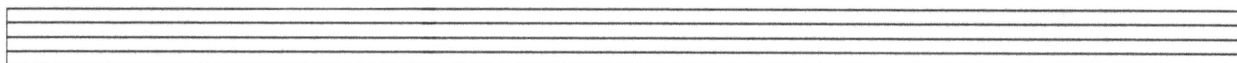

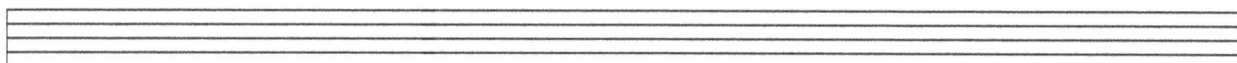

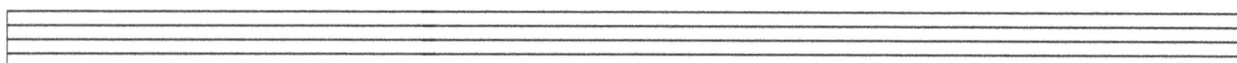

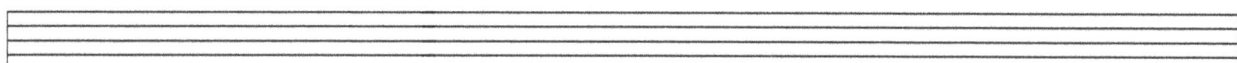

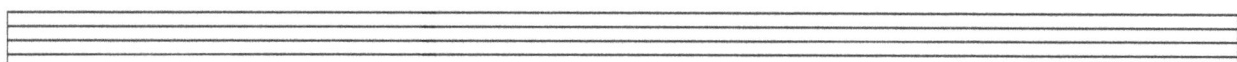

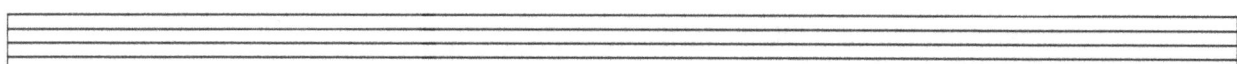

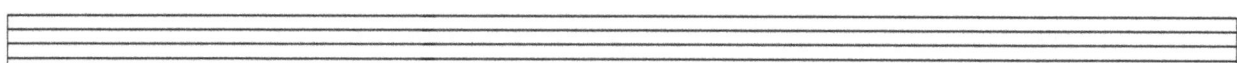

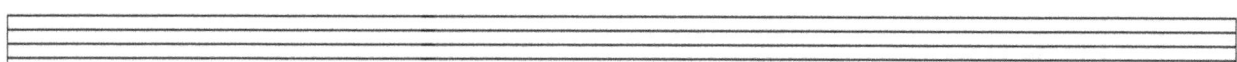

Lesson Two – Rhythm

Refer to:
Contemporary Theory Workbook: Book 1 - Lessons 1, 7, 18, 20 & 21.

CD1 #14   LISTENING

Example One – DUPLE TIME

Part A

CD1 #19

Part B

CD1 #21

CD1 #22   LISTENING

Example Two – TRIPLE TIME

Part A

CD1 #23

Part B

CD1 #25

CD1 #26   LISTENING

Example Three – QUADRUPLE TIME

Part A

CD1 #33

Part B

CD1 #35

Lesson Two – Rhythm
(Continued)

CD1
#36, #37, #38

Question One (a)

Write 2, 3 or 4 to show the number of beats in each bar.

Answers: (1) .... (2) .... (3) ....

CD1 #40

Question One (b)

Using lines, match the type of time signature to the number of beats.

DUPLE	**3**
QUADRUPLE	**2**
TRIPLE	**4**

CD1 #41

LISTENING

Question Two

Use **S** for **SLOW**, **M** for **MODERATE** and **F** for **FAST**.

CD1 #44

Answers: (1) .... (2) .... (3) ....

Question Three

Time signature choices: $\frac{2}{4}$, $\frac{3}{4}$, or $\frac{4}{4}$

CD1 #46

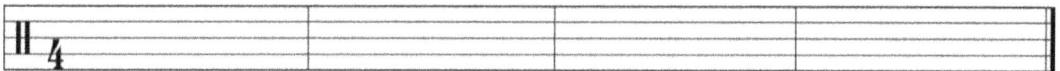

Question Four

CD1 #48

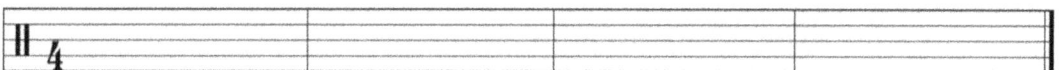

Lesson Three – Pitch

Refer to: Contemporary Theory Primer – Pages 8 & 9
Contemporary Theory Workbook: Book 1 – Lesson 3

A Music Ladder made up of Steps (Seconds)

C Major Scale

CD1 #49

Pairs of Steps

Moving Up   Moving Down

CD1 #52

Question One

Write St↑ or St↓

CD1 #53   Answers: (1) ……….   (2) ……..….   (3) ……..….   (4) …..……

Question Two

Write St↑, St↓ or S (for Same).

CD1 #55   Answers: (1) ……..….   (2) ……..….   (3) ……..….

(4) ……..….   (5) …..……   (6) …..……

Question Three

CD1 #57

Question Four

CD1 #59

Lesson Four – Rhythm

Refer to: Contemporary Theory Primer – Pages 12-15
Contemporary Theory Workbook: Book 1 – Lessons 16-18

TIE – A curved line connecting notes of the same pitch.

NOTE VALUES

Whole note/Semibreve   Half note/Minim   Quarter note/Crotchet

One 4-count note   Two 2-count notes   Four 1-count notes

Move your pen along these strokes in time to the music.

CD2 #1

Example One – Using Four Count Notes

CD2 #3

STAGE ONE: Follow along the printed strokes with the blunt end of your pencil.

STAGE TWO: Place dots under the first stroke in each bar.

STAGE THREE: Connect up the strokes with ties.

STAGE FOUR: Write out the notes in full.

Question One

CD2 # 11

Lesson Four - Rhythm
(Continued)

Example Two – Two count notes

STAGE ONE: Follow along the printed strokes with the blunt end of your pencil.

CD2 #13

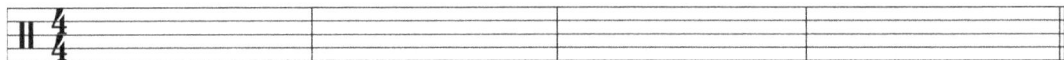
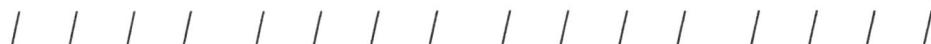

STAGE TWO: Place dots under the first and third strokes in each bar.

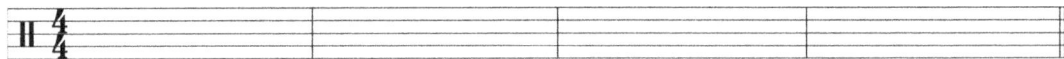

STAGE THREE: Connect up the strokes with ties.

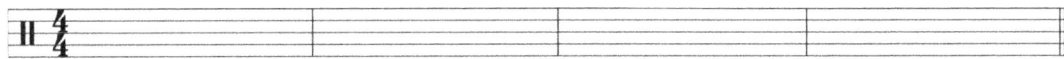

STAGE FOUR: Write out the notes in full.

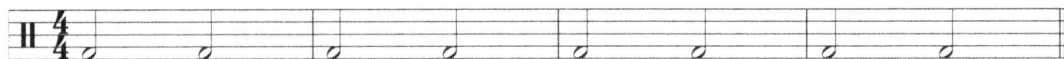
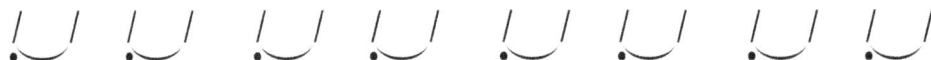

Question Two

CD2 #17

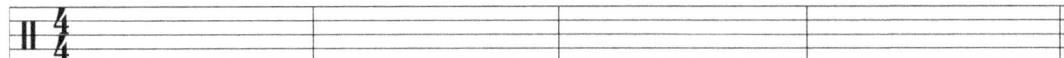

Example Three – One count notes

STAGE ONE: Follow along the printed strokes with the blunt end of your pencil.

CD2 #18

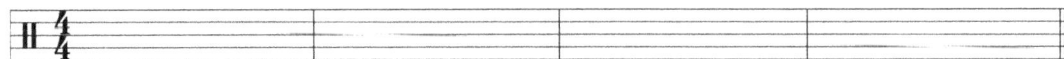

STAGE TWO: Place dots under every stroke in each bar.

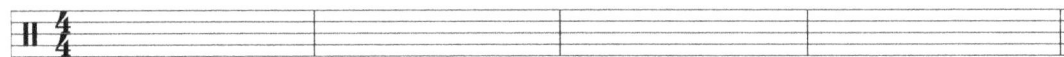

STAGE THREE: Write out the notes in full.

Question Three

CD2 #21

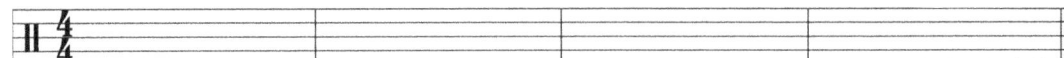

Lesson Four - Rhythm
(Continued)

Example Four – Three count notes

STAGE ONE: Follow along the printed strokes with the blunt end of your pencil.

CD2 # 22

STAGE TWO: Place dots under the first stroke in each bar.

STAGE THREE: Connect up the strokes with ties.

STAGE FOUR: Write out the notes in full.

Question Four

CD2 #26

Example Five – Music in $\frac{2}{4}$ time

The types of notes you will find in 2/4 time in Set One of this series are two-count notes and one-count notes.
Below are two examples of music in 2/4 time.

5(a)

CD2 #27

5(b)

CD2 #28

Music with mixtures of note values will be heard in Set One.

Lesson Five – Pitch

Part A

C Major Scale

First Five Notes

| La | La | La | La | La | La | La | La | La |
| 1 | St Up | St Up | St Up | St Up | St Dn | St Dn | St Dn | St Dn |

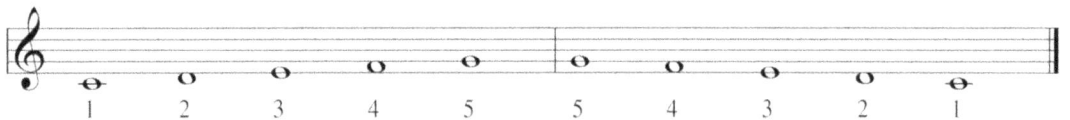

| 1 | 2 | 3 | 4 | 5 | 5 | 4 | 3 | 2 | 1 |

REPEATED NOTES – SAMES or Primes or Unison

| 1 | Same | 1 | 1 | **or** 1 | Same | 1 | 1 |

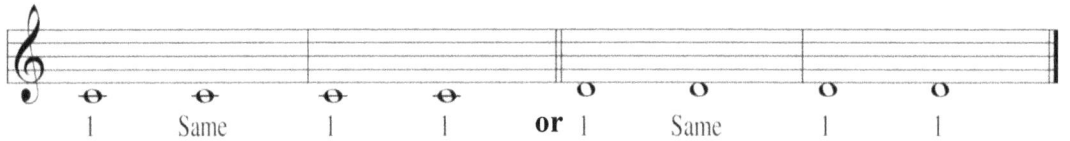

STEPS or SECONDS

Melodic Steps   Harmonic Steps

| 1 | Step | 1 | Step | **or** 1 | 2 | 2 | 1 |

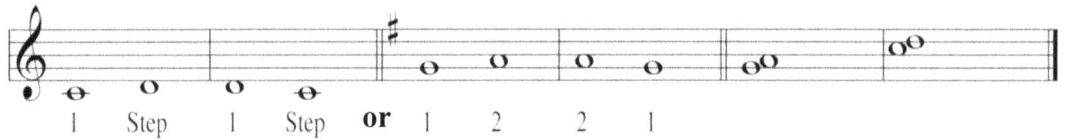

Said the Kind Kangaroo

1   2   etc

Write out the first two bars of any other songs which begin with a **Step**.

LISTENING – Harmonic **Steps** and **Skips**

Lesson Five - Pitch
(Continued)

SKIPS or **THIRDS**

Melodic Skips   Harmonic Skips

1 2 3   1   3 **or** 3 2 1   3   1

Michael Row The Boat Ashore

1   3

Write out the first two bars of any songs which begin with a **Skip**.

Frere Jacques

1   2   3   1

Part B

SKIP-PLUS-ONES or **FOURTHS**

Melodic Skip-Plus-Ones   Harmonic Skip-Plus-Ones

1 2 3 4   1   4   4 3 2 1   4   1

Auld Lang Syne   **Two Fat Gentlemen**

4th   4th

Write out the first two bars of any other songs which begin with a **Skip-Plus-One**.

Lesson 5 - Pitch
(Continued)

JUMPS or **FIFTHS**

Melodic Jumps   Harmonic Jumps

1 2 3 4 5 1   5   **or**   5 4 3 2 1   5   1

Twinkle Twinkle Little Star

1   1   5

Write out the first two bars of any songs which begin with a **Jump**.

Outlining the **JUMP** using **SKIPS** which make up the **MAJOR CHORD**

1   3   5   1   5   5   3   1   5   1

Michael Row the Boat Ashore   **Love Somebody**

1   3   5   1   3   5

Write out the first two bars of any other songs which begin with two **Skips**.

Lesson 6 - Rhythm

Question One

CD2 #54

‖ 4/4   / / / /   / / / /   / / / /   / / / /

Question Two

CD2 #55

‖ 4/4   / / / /   / / / /   / / / /   / / / /

Question Three

CD2 #56

‖ 4/4   / / / /   / / / /   / / / /   / / / /

Question Four

CD2 #57

‖ 4/4   / / / /   / / / /   / / / /   / / / /

Question Five

CD2 #58

‖ 3/4   / / /   / / /   / / /   / / /

Question Six

CD2 #59

‖ 3/4   / / /   / / /   / / /   / / /

Question Seven

CD2 #60

‖ 2/4   / /   / /   / /   / /

Question Eight

CD2 #61

‖ 2/4   / /   / /   / /   / /

Terminology Used In This Course

INTERVALS

An **interval** is the distance between two notes.

Same or Unison

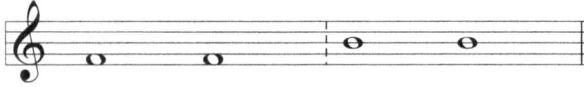

Space - Space   *or*   Line-Line

Steps or Seconds

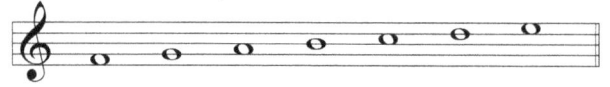

Alternate Lines and Spaces

Skips or Thirds

Line to Line   *or*   Space to Space

Skip-Plus-One or Fourth

Space to Line   *or*   Line to Space

Jumps or Fifths

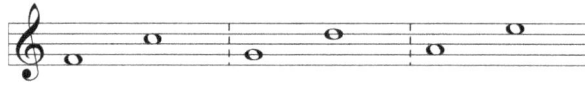

Space to Space *or* Line to Line

Time values of Notes and Rests

In music, we use **notes** to indicate **sounds**, and **rests** to indicate periods of **silence**.

Notes	American Name	British Name	Duration
o	Whole note	Semibreve	4 counts
♩	Half note	Minim	2 counts
♩	Quarter note	Crotchet	1 count
♪	Eighth note	Quaver	½ count

Rests	American Name	British Name	Duration
▬	Whole rest	Semibreve rest	4 counts
▬	Half rest	Minim rest	2 counts
𝄽	Quarter rest	Crotchet rest	1 count
𝄾	Eighth rest	Quaver rest	½ count

Contemporary Aural Course

Preparatory for beginners

By Margaret S. Brandman

Answer Pages

Answer Page - Preparatory

Lesson 1

Question 1:   (1) H   (2) L   (3) M   (4) H

Question 2:

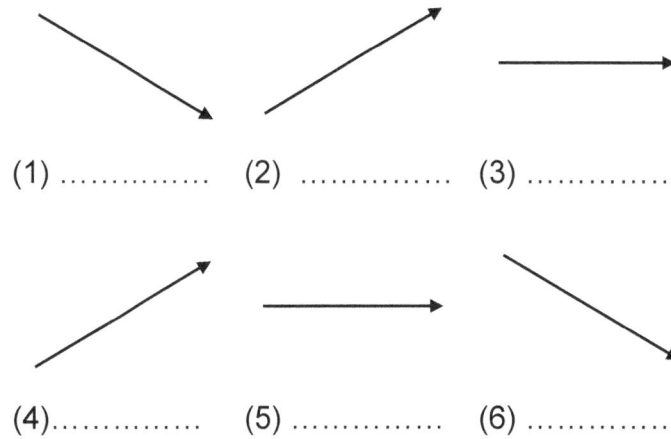

(1) ....   (2) ....   (3) ....

(4)...............   (5) ....   (6) ....

Question 3:   (1) L   (2) H   (3) H   (4) L

Question 4:   (1) H   (2) S   (3) L   (4) S   (5) L   (6) S

Lesson 2

Question 1 (a):   (1) 3   (2) 2   (3) 4

Question 1 (b):

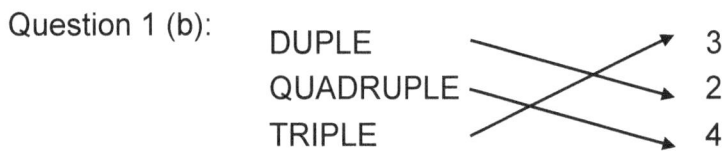

Question 2:   (1) F   (2) S   (3) M

Question 3:

Question 4:

Answer Page - Preparatory

Lesson 3

Question 1:   (1) St↑   (2) St↓   (3) St↓   (4) St↑

Question 2:   (1) St↓   (2) St↑   (3) S   (4) St↑   (5) S   (6) St↓

Question 3:

Question 4:

Lesson 4

Question 1:

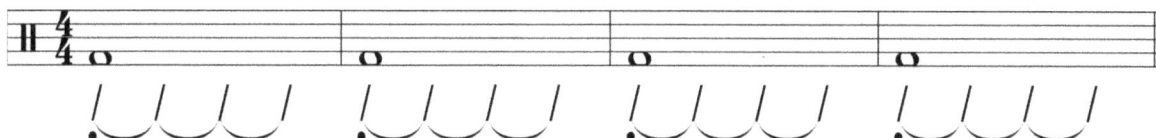

Question 2:

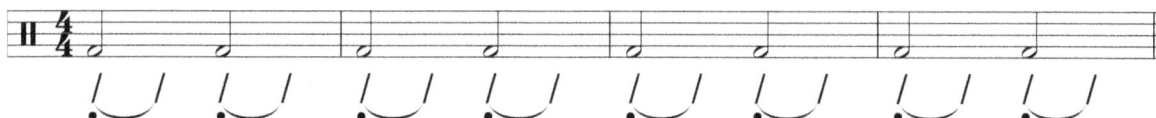

Question 3:

Question 4:

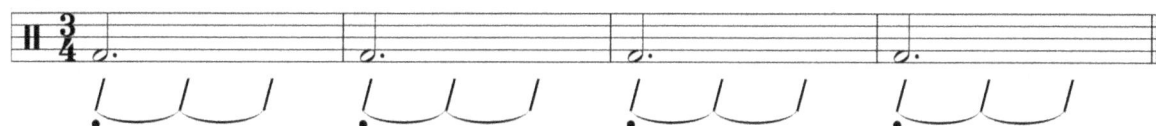

Lesson 5 - No answers needed.

Answer Page - Preparatory

Lesson 6

Question 1

Question 2

Question 3

Question 4

Question 5

Question 6

Question 7

Question 8

www.ingramcontent.com/pod-product-compliance
Lightning Source LLC
Chambersburg PA
CBHW081601040426
42448CB00013B/3153